MENSA®
PRESENTS
PUZZLE CHALLENGE
for KIDS

THIS IS A CARLTON BOOK

Text copyright © 1995 British Mensa Limited
Design and artwork copyright © 1995 Carlton Books Limited

This edition published by Barnes & Noble Inc.,
by arrangement with Carlton Books Ltd

2002 Barnes & Noble Books

ISBN 0-7607-0432-5

10 9 8 7 6 5 4 3

Printed in Italy

MENSA
PRESENTS
PUZZLE CHALLENGE for KIDS

Carolyn Skitt

BARNES
&NOBLE
BOOKS
NEW YORK

CONTENTS

INTRODUCTION

You didn't buy this book yourself, did you? I guessed as much. This is the kind of book that gets bought as a present by a well-meaning relative on the grounds that it's "good for you". Well, I have good news: the last laugh is yours, this book is FUN. Maybe it's not the sort of fun where people get the wrong answer and fall into a tank of green slime (we're working on that one). Even so, you'll find that after you've done one or two puzzles you will be seriously hooked. Your mind will become locked in a battle of wits with the puzzle writer and you will never be able to give up until victory is yours.

Talking of puzzle writers, this book is the work of my colleagues Carolyn Skitt and Bobby Raikhy. Carolyn is the power-house of Mensa's puzzle writing department. Her work appears in countless newspapers and magazines. Though you may not have seen her name (puzzle writers don't get much recognition) you will probably have tried her puzzles before. What can I say about Bobby? Cool, debonair and uncrowned king of DTP should just about cover it.

Before trying to race through the puzzles you may find it useful to read the author's help notes on the opposite page. And when you have finished the puzzles in this book and are desperate for more, why not join Mensa? For details and a home test write to your nearest Mensa organization. British Mensa Limited is at Mensa House, St John's Square, Wolverhampton, WV2 4AH, England. American Mensa Limited is at 2626 E 14th Street, Brooklyn, New York 11235-3992, USA, or contact Mensa International, 15 The Ivories, 628 Northampton Street, London N1 2NY, England who will be happy to put you in touch with your own national Mensa.

Robert Allen
Editorial Director
Mensa Publications

AUTHOR'S NOTES

I hope that you enjoy working through these puzzles as much as we have enjoyed compiling them. I would like to thank Bobby Raikhy and the staff at Mensa headquarters for their support and Carlton Books, who have made this publication possible.

You will find that some of the puzzles are particularly devious so here are a few clues which you may find useful:

1. Where words are converted to numbers look for Roman numeral values (I = 1, V = 5, X = 10, L = 50, C = 100, D = 500 and M = 1000). Also look for consonants and vowels having a value or alpha-numeric values, i.e., A = 1, B = 2 etc.

2. Average speeds can be calculated by dividing the total distance by the total time. If no time is given assume that the outward journey is completed in one hour and calculate the return time.

3. Intermeshing gears: calculate the number of teeth movements of the largest wheel. The others will then divide into this to give the number of revolutions of each of the wheels. The largest wheel moves clockwise, therefore the second largest will move anti-clockwise (or counterclockwise), the third will move clockwise and the fourth anti-clockwise (or counterclockwise).

4. In the cog questions look for the lowest common denominator.

5. With any of the recycling questions remember to keep dividing and using up all of the new remainders each time.

6. Where two or three words are merged together do not assume that all the words follow the same direction.

I hope these notes are helpful to you and GOOD LUCK!

PUZZLE 1

Move from square to touching square, including diagonals, to discover the longest possible country name from these letters.

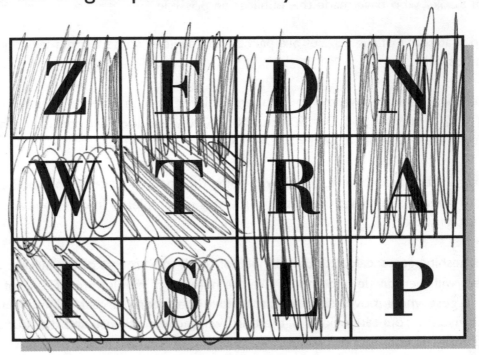

SEE ANSWER 64

PUZZLE 2

What time should the fourth clock show?

SEE ANSWER 1

PUZZLE 3

What numbers are missing from these series?

A

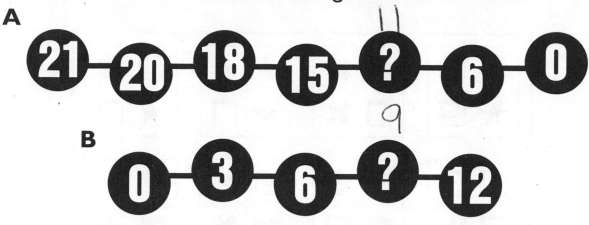

B

SEE ANSWER 56

PUZZLE 4

All these children's ages relate to their names. Can you work out how old Andrew is?

Harry 8
Ronald 18
Nicola 14
Andrew ?
Caroline 3

SEE ANSWER 9

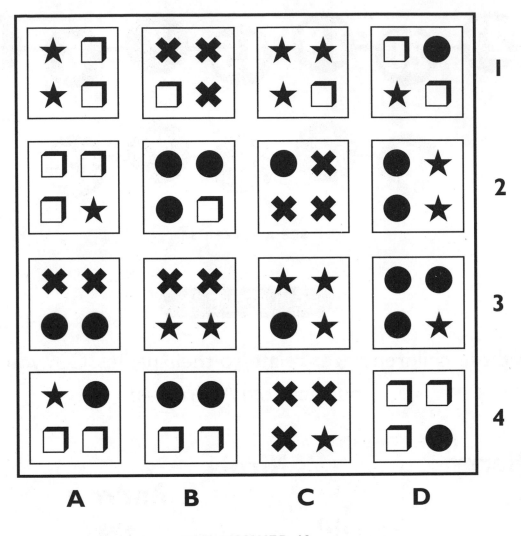

PUZZLE 5

Which two boxes in this diagram are alike?

SEE ANSWER 48

PUZZLE 6

Underline two words in the brackets which have the same relationship as the two words before the brackets.

A EAT FORK (Knife, <u>Food</u>, Table, Pencil, Draw)
B COLD TEPID (Wet, Frozen, Solid, <u>Hot</u>, <u>Warm</u>)

SEE ANSWER 17

LEVEL ● EASY

Which of the numbers in each line is the odd one out?

A 6 12 18 26 30 36

B 135 246 357 468 689

SEE ANSWER 40

PUZZLE 8

Start at the far left circle and move – to the right only – along the lines to the far right circle, collecting the numbers and the ovals as you go. An oval is worth –37. How many routes give 152?

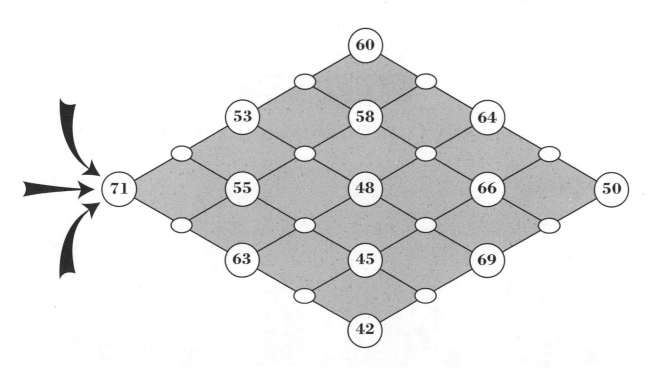

SEE ANSWER 25

PUZZLE 9

Arrange the pieces to form a square where the
numbers read the same horizontally and vertically.
What will the finished square look like?

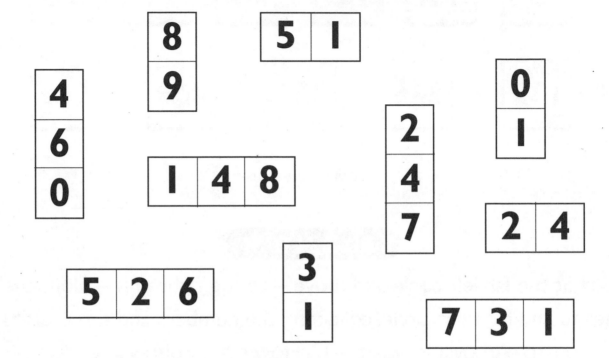

SEE ANSWER 32

PUZZLE 10

Should A, B, C, or D come next in this series?

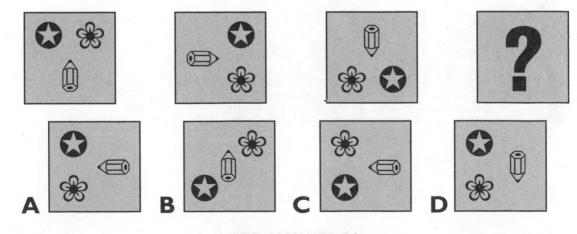

SEE ANSWER 33

PUZZLE 11

Four of these animals have something in common. Which is the odd one out? (Clue: think diets)

SEE ANSWER 24

PUZZLE 12

I was five times as old as my sister five years ago, and I am three times older than her now. How old am I?

SEE ANSWER 41

PUZZLE 13

What number should replace the question mark?

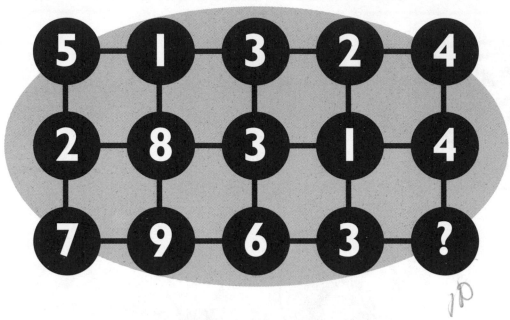

SEE ANSWER 16

PUZZLE 14

Remove eight of these straight lines to leave only two squares.
How can this be done?

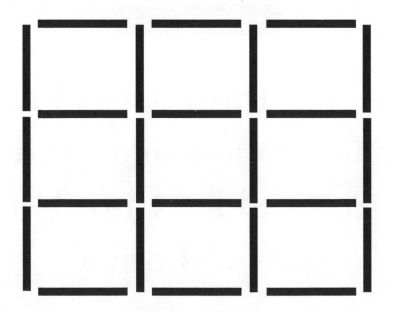

SEE ANSWER 49

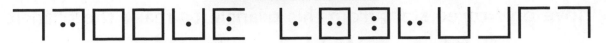

Above is the code for SUMMER HOLIDAYS.
What is written on each line below?

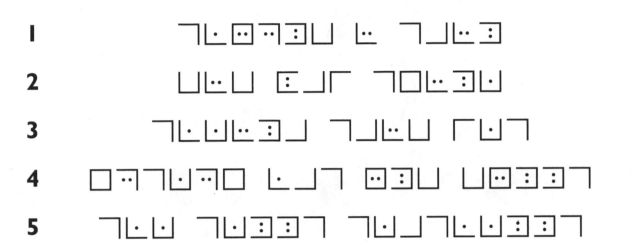

1

2

3

4

5

SEE ANSWER 8

PUZZLE 16

Each shape in the diagram has a value. Work out the values to discover what number should replace the question mark.

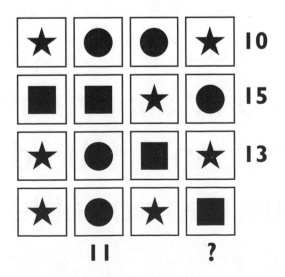

10

15

13

11   ?

SEE ANSWER 57

Move only three stars from this triangle to make the triangle turn upside down. Which three should be moved?

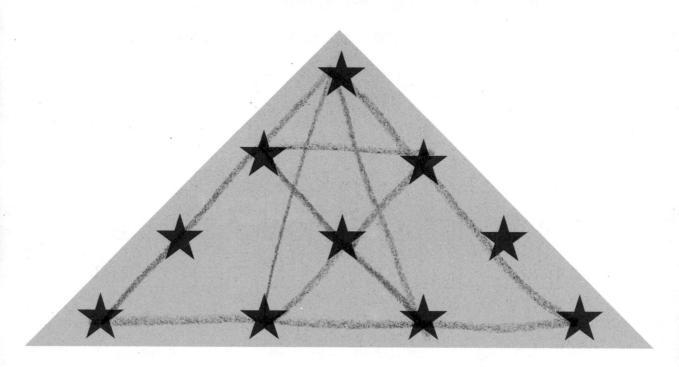

SEE ANSWER 63

PUZZLE 18

Draw four equal triangles using only six straight lines. How can this be done? There are two possible answers.

SEE ANSWER 2

LEVEL · EASY

16

Which one of the following numbers is the odd one out?

SEE ANSWER 55

PUZZLE 20

There is a different pattern on each side of the box. Which of these is not a view of the same box?

A

B

C

D

SEE ANSWER 10

LEVEL • EASY

17

In row A-A there are three rabbits. Another three rabbits are in row C-C. In row B-B there are two rabbits. How many rows are there of three rabbits and how many of two? Remove three rabbits and arrange the remaining six in three rows of three rabbits each. How can this be done?

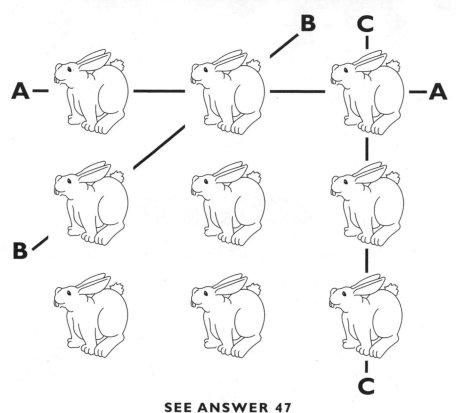

SEE ANSWER 47

PUZZLE 22

Which of the following foods is the odd one out?

Pizza   Spaghetti

Boiled Egg   Penne

SEE ANSWER 18

18

LEVEL · EASY

This is Morse Code, invented by Samuel Morse in 1838.

A	·—	G	——·	M	——	S	···
B	—···	H	····	N	—·	T	—
C	—·—·	I	··	O	———	U	··—
D	—··	J	·———	P	·——·	V	···—
E	·	K	—·—	Q	——·—	W	·——
F	··—·	L	·—··	R	·—·	X	—··—
						Y	—·——
						Z	——··

Can you work out these secret messages?

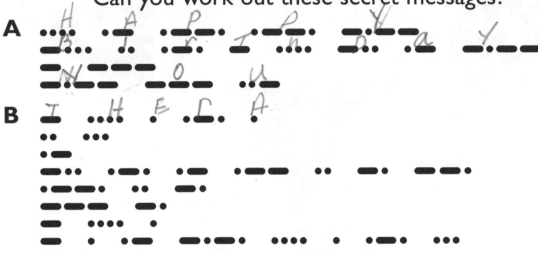

A ···· ·— ·——· ·——· ·· —· ——— ·——· ·—— —··· ·· ·—· ——· —··· ·— ·—·· ——— ··—— —··· ·— —·——

B ·· ···· · ·—··

SEE ANSWER 39

SEE ANSWER 39

PUZZLE 24

What time should the fourth clock show?

SEE ANSWER 26

LEVEL • EASY

19

PUZZLE 25

What number should replace the question mark
in the fourth triangle?

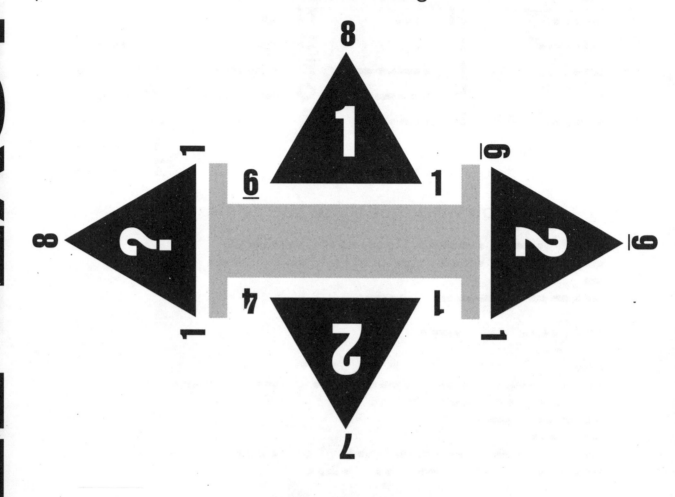

SEE ANSWER 31

PUZZLE 26

Look carefully at these words.
There is something fishy about them. What is it?

CARPET CODES SPIKED SOLEMN

SEE ANSWER 34

20

PUZZLE 27

Should box A, B, C or D come next in this series?

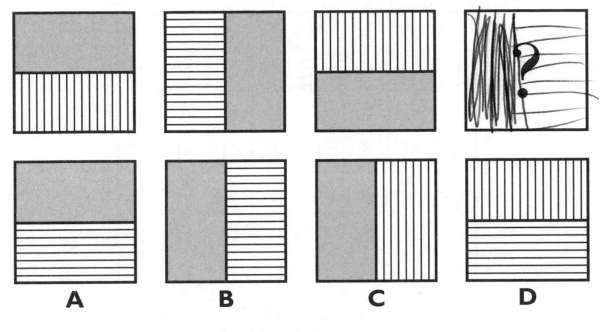

A   **B**   **C**   **D**

SEE ANSWER 23

PUZZLE 28

What is missing from these series?

A 6 15 24 ? 42

B 1 4 9 ? 25

SEE ANSWER 42

21

PUZZLE 29

Can you find the 20 creatures in the wordsearch below?

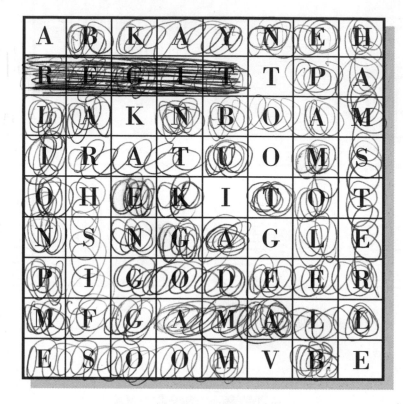

A	B	K	A	Y	N	E	H
R	E	G	I	T	T	P	A
L	A	K	N	B	O	A	M
I	R	A	T	U	O	M	S
O	H	E	K	I	T	O	T
N	S	N	G	A	G	L	E
P	I	G	O	D	E	E	R
M	F	G	A	M	A	L	L
E	S	O	O	M	V	B	E

Ape   Deer   Goat   Llama   Pig
Badger   Dog   Hamster   Mink   Rat
Bear   Fish   Hen   Mole   Tiger
Boa   Gnu   Lion   Moose   Yak

SEE ANSWER 15

PUZZLE 30

Which of these is not a view of the same three sides of a box?

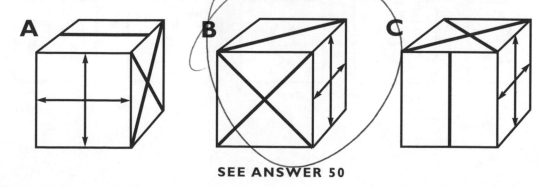

A   **B**   **C**

SEE ANSWER 50

Which of the numbers on these balloons is the odd one out?

A
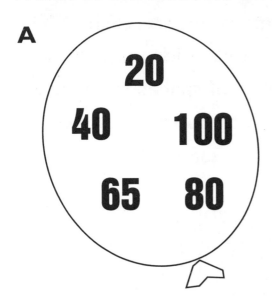

B
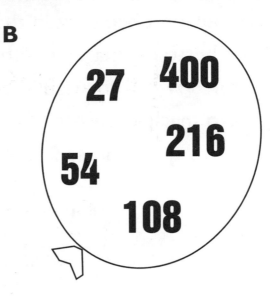

SEE ANSWER 7

PUZZLE 32

Which two boxes are alike?

	1	2	3	4
D	★▲ ▲★	++ ▲★	●● ▲★	▲ +★ ▲
C	★ ★▲ +	▲ ▲● ★	++ ●●	★▲ ●★
B	●▲ +★	+ +▲ ▲	+ ★● +	● ▲+ ●
A	+ ▲● +	★ ★★ +	★▲ ●+	★ ++● ★

SEE ANSWER 58

LEVEL • EASY

23

There is only one way to open this safe. You must press each button once only, in the correct order, to reach OPEN. Each button is marked with a direction, U for up, L for left, D for down, R for right. The number of spaces to move is also marked on each button. Which button must you press first to open the safe?

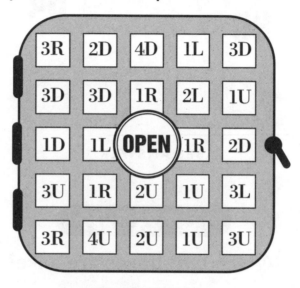

SEE ANSWER 3

PUZZLE 34

On this strange signpost how far should it be to Aberdeen?

Edinburgh	50
Cardiff	30
Bristol	20
Aberdeen	?
Ipswich	90

SEE ANSWER 62

LEVEL · EASY

Replace the vowels in each of the following to form words.
Which words are the odd ones out?

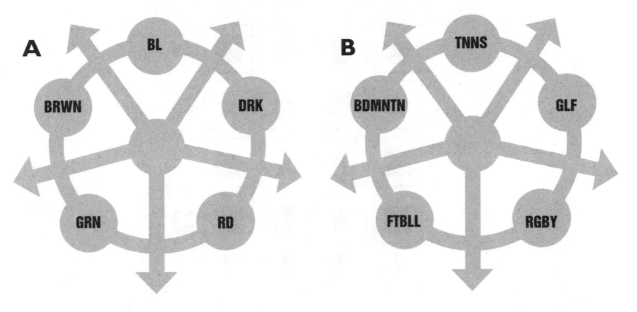

A

BL
BRWN
DRK
GRN
RD

B

TNNS
BDMNTN
GLF
FTBLL
RGBY

SEE ANSWER II

PUZZLE 36

What number should replace the question mark?

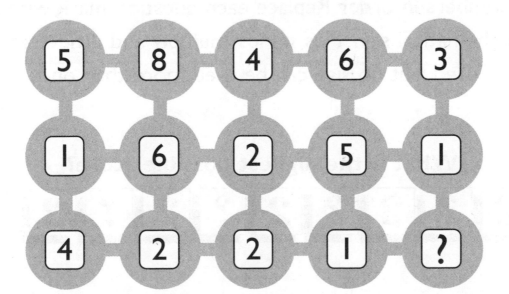

5	8	4	6	3
1	6	2	5	1
4	2	2	1	?

SEE ANSWER 54

LEVEL • EASY

Each shape in this diagram has a value. Work out the values to discover what numbers should replace the question marks.

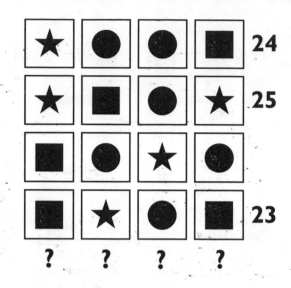

SEE ANSWER 19

PUZZLE 38

Assume you are using a basic calculator and press these numbers in order. Replace each question mark with a mathematical sign. Plus, minus, multiply and divide can be used, but no sign can be used more than once.

What is the highest possible score?

SEE ANSWER 46

PUZZLE 39

Which route should the bear take to get to the woods?

SEE ANSWER 27

PUZZLE 40

Which of these discs is the odd one out?

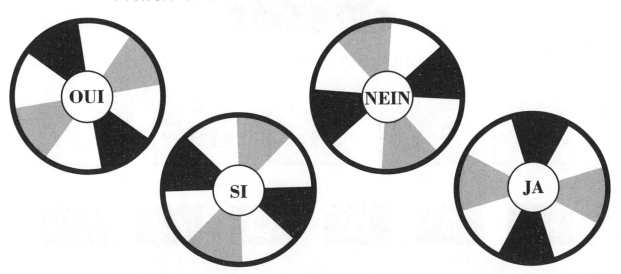

OUI

NEIN

SI

JA

SEE ANSWER 38

PUZZLE 41

The wordframe, when filled with the correct letters will give the name of a city in England and Alabama. The letters are arranged in the coded square. There are two possible letters to fill each square of the wordframe, one correct, one incorrect.

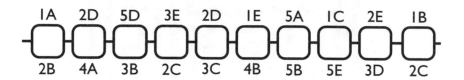

1A   2D   5D   3E   2D   1E   5A   1C   2E   1B

2B   4A   3B   2C   3C   4B   5B   5E   3D   2C

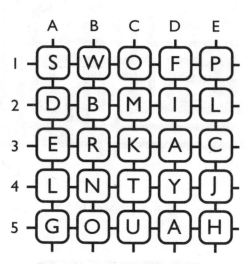

	A	B	C	D	E
1	S	W	O	F	P
2	D	B	M	I	L
3	E	R	K	A	C
4	L	N	T	Y	J
5	G	O	U	A	H

SEE ANSWER 35

PUZZLE 42

Which of the following numbers is the odd one out?

A   313   454   262   695   727

B   4   8   10   32   64   128

SEE ANSWER 30

Assume you are using a basic calculator and press these numbers in order. Replace each question mark with a mathematical sign. Plus, minus, multiply and divide can be used, but no sign can be used more than once.

In which order must they be used?

 = 2

SEE ANSWER 43

PUZZLE 44

Arrange the pieces to form a square where the numbers read the same horizontally and vertically.

SEE ANSWER 22

LEVEL • EASY

Start at the far left circle and move, to the rightly only, along the lines to the far right circle, collecting numbers and ovals as you go. Each oval has a value of –41. How many routes give 0?

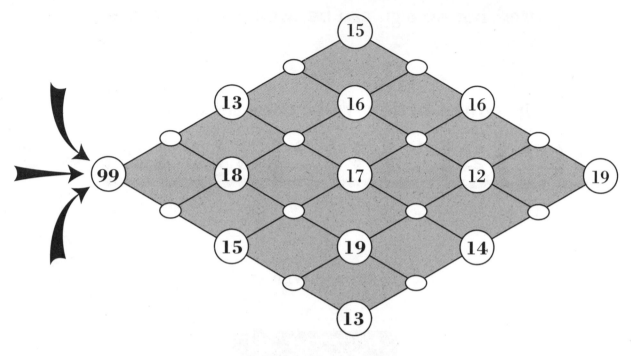

SEE ANSWER 51

PUZZLE 46

What number should replace the question mark?

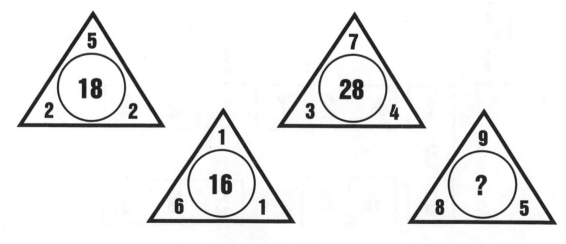

SEE ANSWER 14

LEVEL • EASY

PUZZLE 47

Here is an unusual safe. Each button must be pressed once only, in the correct order, to reach OPEN. The direction to move, i for in, o for out, c for clockwise, and a for anti-clockwise (counterclockwise) is marked on each button. The number of spaces to move is also shown on each button. Which button is the first you must press to open the safe?

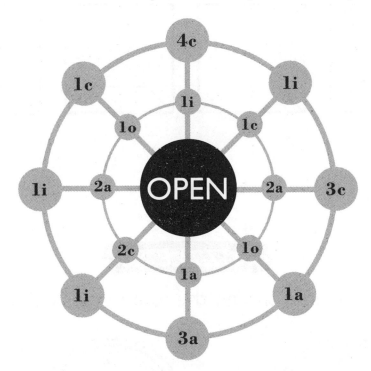

SEE ANSWER 59

PUZZLE 48

Replace the vowels in each of the lines to form words. Which word in each line is the odd one out?

A **SLVR   BRSS   GLD   STL   MRLD**

B **BGL   HND   TRRR   LBRDR   FX**

SEE ANSWER 6

PUZZLE 49

Should A, B, C or D come next in the series?

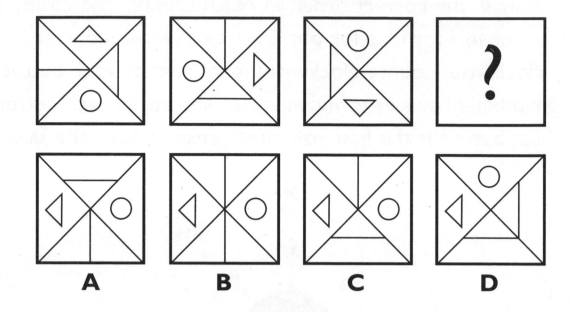

A   **B**   **C**   **D**

SEE ANSWER 4

PUZZLE 50

What time should the fourth clock show?

SEE ANSWER 61

Choose the odd one out on each line and write its initial in the space alongside. When completed these initials will give a word reading downwards. What is the word?

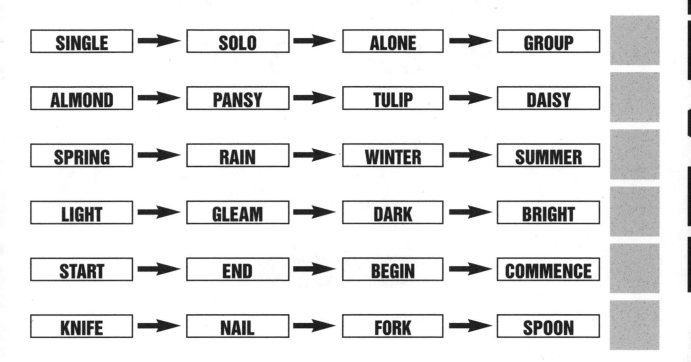

SINGLE → SOLO → ALONE → GROUP

ALMOND → PANSY → TULIP → DAISY

SPRING → RAIN → WINTER → SUMMER

LIGHT → GLEAM → DARK → BRIGHT

START → END → BEGIN → COMMENCE

KNIFE → NAIL → FORK → SPOON

SEE ANSWER 12

Move from square to touching square – including diagonals – to discover the longest possible word from these letters.

A	G	M	O
R	N	D	T
Y	R	E	H

SEE ANSWER 53

LEVEL • EASY

PUZZLE 53

What number should replace the question mark?

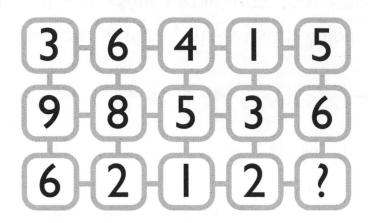

SEE ANSWER 20

PUZZLE 54

Which two boxes in this diagram are alike?

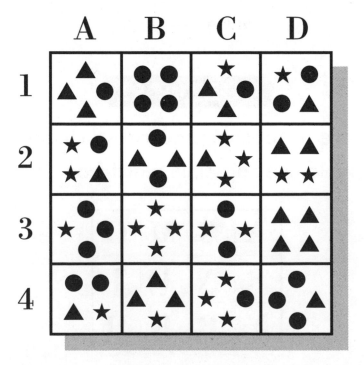

SEE ANSWER 45

Each shape in this diagram has a value. Work out the values to discover what number should replace the question mark.

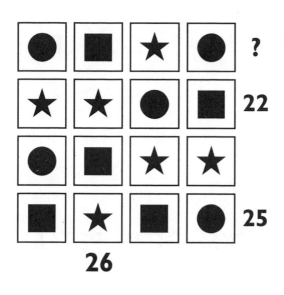

26

SEE ANSWER 28

The fares for these train rides all relate to the place names in England. What is the fare to Oxford ?

Bath £17
Brighton £34
London £24
Taunton £26
Oxford ?

SEE ANSWER 37

LEVEL • EASY

Rearrange each group of letters to form a word.
Which word is the odd one out?

A TROPICA   CHEAP   CUTTLEE   GNOMA   MILE

B NIOMS   AILS   DRAICHR   KREED   ONCIL

C PONOS   PICKSHOCT   PETAL   FROK   FINKE

SEE ANSWER 36

PUZZLE 58

Which of the following is not a view of the same
three sides of a box?

A **B** **C**

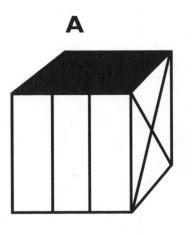
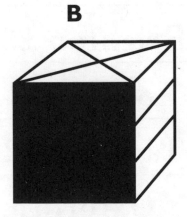

SEE ANSWER 29

LEVEL • EASY

PUZZLE 59

The distances on this fictitious signpost relate to the states' placenames. How far is it to Kentucky?

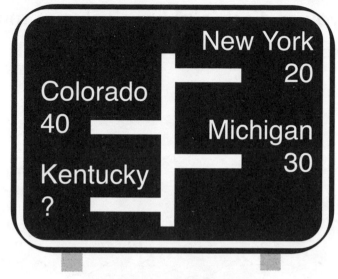

New York
20

Colorado
40

Michigan
30

Kentucky
?

SEE ANSWER 44

PUZZLE 60

These jumbled letters spell the names of two tennis stars. Who are they?

SEE ANSWER 21

Start at the far left circle and move – to the right only – along the lines to the far right circle, collecting the numbers and the ovals as you go. Each oval has a value of minus 13. What are the minimum and maximum totals possible?

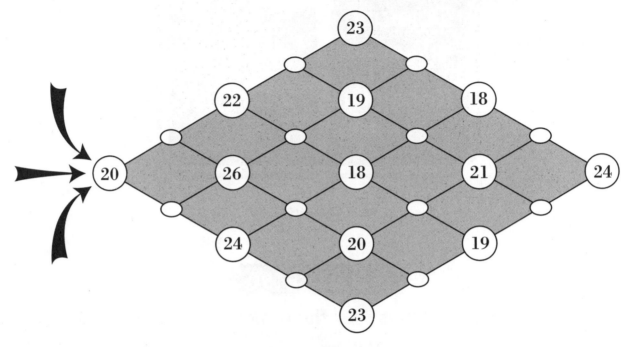

SEE ANSWER 52

PUZZLE 62

Which of the boxes continues this sequence and replaces the question mark?

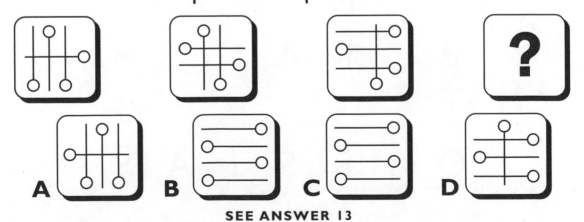

SEE ANSWER 13

If you go from square to touching square – including diagonals – which country will you find using all the letters only once?

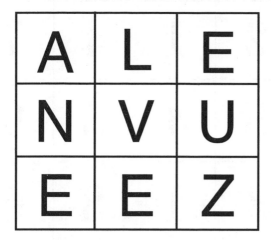

SEE ANSWER 60

On this unusual dartboard how many different ways are there to score 30 with three darts? Every dart must land in a segment (more than one dart may land in each), and all must score. The same three scores in a different order do not count as another way.

SEE ANSWER 5

LEVEL • EASY

PUZZLE 1

What number should replace the question mark?

2	1	4	7
5	4	5	9
3	1	8	6
8	3	?	4

SEE ANSWER 60

PUZZLE 2

The minute and hour hands move separately on these strange clocks. What time should the fourth clock show?

1   2   3   4

SEE ANSWER 5

 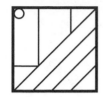 

Should A, B, C or D come next in this series?

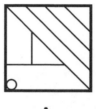  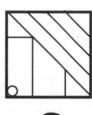 

A   B   C   D

SEE ANSWER 52

PUZZLE 4

Each shape in the diagram has a value. Work out the values to discover what number should replace the question mark.

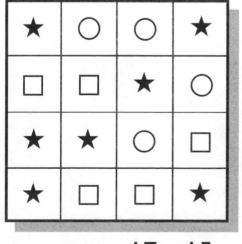

SEE ANSWER 13

LEVEL • MEDIUM

41

PUZZLE 5

What number should replace the question mark?

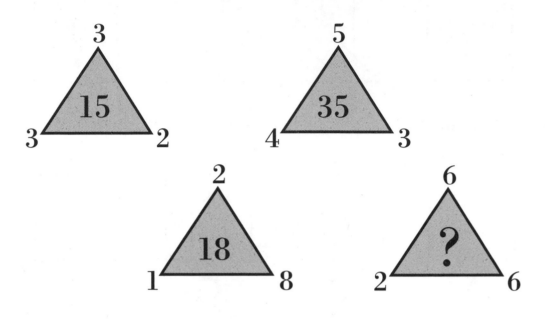

SEE ANSWER 44

PUZZLE 6

What number is missing from this series?

2   3   5   ?   11

SEE ANSWER 21

PUZZLE 7

The value of each instrument in a music store in Chicago follows a certain logic. How much does a keyboard cost?

Guitar $39

Trombone $49

Drums $28

Oboe $29

Keyboard $?

SEE ANSWER 36

PUZZLE 8

What number should replace the question mark?

8	1	2	4
6	1	3	7
9	1	7	8
5	1	4	9
8	?	?	8

SEE ANSWER 29

PUZZLE 9

What time should the fourth clock show?

1   2   3   4

SEE ANSWER 28

PUZZLE 10

Each shape in the diagram has a value. Work out the values to discover what number should replace the question mark.

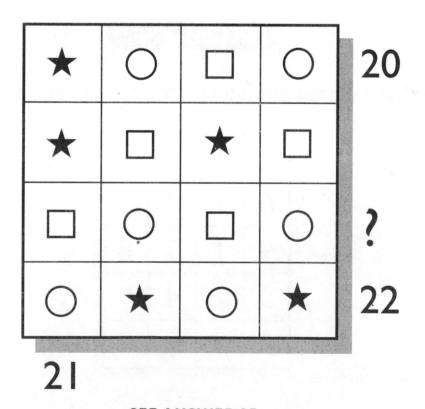

SEE ANSWER 37

PUZZLE 11

4C	1E	5B	1B	3C	4B	3E	1C	4A
1A	3D	3A	4E	2D	5A	4D	2B	5E

The wordframe above, when filled with the correct letters, will give the name of a composer. The letters are arranged in the coded square. There are two possible letters to fill each square of the wordframe, one correct, the other is incorrect each time. Who is the composer?

	A	B	C	D	E
1	W	T	E	D	E
2	F	C	R	H	P
3	E	U	A	I	U
4	K	M	B	V	S
5	O	L	J	G	N

SEE ANSWER 20

PUZZLE 12

What number is missing from this series?

1   3   6   10   (?)   21

SEE ANSWER 45

PUZZLE 13

What number should replace the question mark?

6	2	4
9	4	5
8	7	1
4	1	?

SEE ANSWER 12

PUZZLE 14

Each shape has a value. Scales 1 and 2 are in perfect balance.
How many squares are needed to balance scale 3?

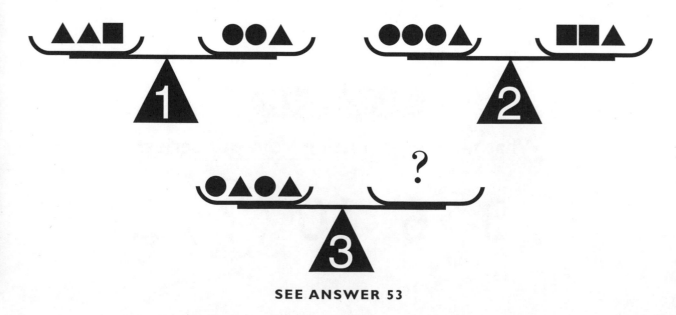

SEE ANSWER 53

PUZZLE 15

The price to enter animal enclosures in a wildlife park is shown below. How much is it to see the elephants?

Aardvark free

Bear $3

Lion $3

Dolphin $11

Elephant $?

SEE ANSWER 4

PUZZLE 16

Start at the far left circle and move – to the right only – along the lines to the far right circle, collecting numbers and ovals as you go. Each oval has a value of –20. What is the most common score?

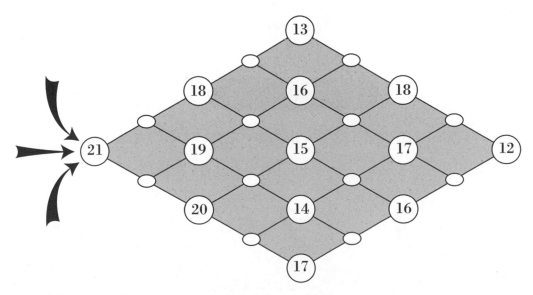

SEE ANSWER 61

PUZZLE 17

Arrange the pieces to form a square where the numbers
read the same horizontally and vertically.
What will the finished square look like?

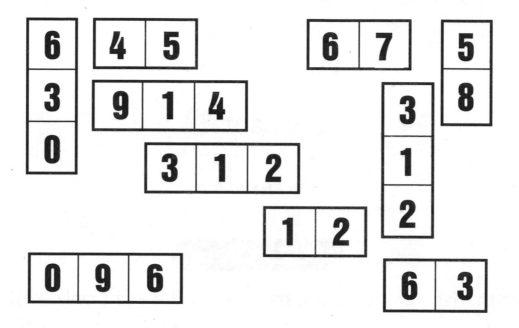

SEE ANSWER 56

PUZZLE 18

What number is missing from this series?

1   3   7   (?)   31

SEE ANSWER 1

PUZZLE 19

What is the price on the ticket on the waistcoat in this unusual store in Sydney?

Socks $1.20

Trousers $2.55

Shirt $1.20

Jumper $1.80

Waistcoat $?

SEE ANSWER 48

PUZZLE 20

Three artists, Michaelangelo, Constable and Leonardo Da Vinci are hidden in this coded message. Who are the five artists below them?

1
2
3
4
5
6

SEE ANSWER 9

49

PUZZLE 21

A cyclist rides at 16 miles per hour before returning over the same journey at 10 miles per hour. What is the cyclist's average speed over the total journey?

SEE ANSWER 40

PUZZLE 22

Move from square to touching square – including diagonals – and, using all the letters, find a musical instrument.

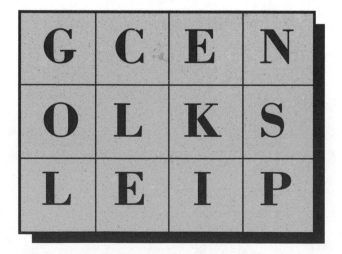

SEE ANSWER 17

The hands on these clocks move in a strange but logical way.
What is the time on the fourth clock?

SEE ANSWER 32

PUZZLE 24

At the fair, you have to throw three pebbles to land on these markers. Each pebble must count and more than one can land on the same marker, but the same three markers in a different order does not count. How many ways are there to score 55?

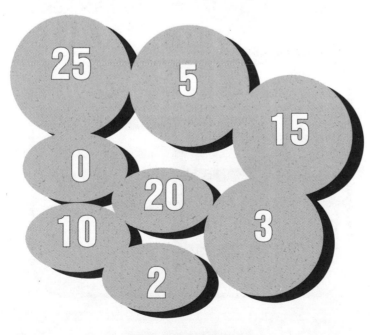

SEE ANSWER 25

LEVEL • MEDIUM

PUZZLE 25

Which two boxes contain exactly the same letters?
(They may be in a different order.)

	A	B	C	D
1	B B A A	A B C A A C	A A A A	B B A C
2	B B A B	A A A B	C C B B	A A C
3	C C C C	A B C	A C C	B B B C
4	B C C A	A A A C	B B B B	C A C B

SEE ANSWER 24

PUZZLE 26

This strange signpost shows the distances to motor-racing destinations. How far is it to Hockenheim?

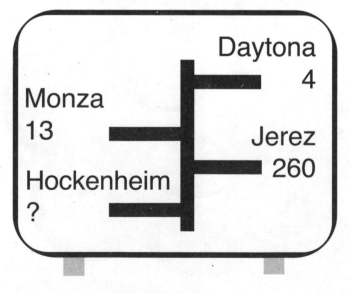

Daytona
4

Monza
13

Jerez
260

Hockenheim
?

SEE ANSWER 33

In this grid you will find 10 American states, written in straight lines with no letters missed out or spaces between the letters. The names are written forward or backward, up, down, across or diagonally. Can you find them all? The states are:

Alaska   California   Montana   New Mexico   Texas
Arizona   Colorado   Nevada   Oregon   Wyoming

N	B	W	R	Y	A	V	M	D	A
X	E	J	V	D	H	A	O	I	C
H	B	W	A	C	R	K	N	A	F
Y	D	V	M	I	T	R	T	K	G
K	E	F	Z	E	O	W	A	S	N
N	Q	O	X	F	X	Q	N	A	I
B	N	A	I	G	P	I	A	L	M
A	S	L	H	C	B	F	C	A	O
P	A	J	N	O	G	E	R	O	Y
C	O	L	O	R	A	D	O	G	W

SEE ANSWER 41

53

PUZZLE 28

In her piggy bank, Jane has $5.24. The sum is made up of an equal number of four coins from 1c, 5c, 10c, 25c, 50c and $1, Which four coins does she have and how many of each of them?

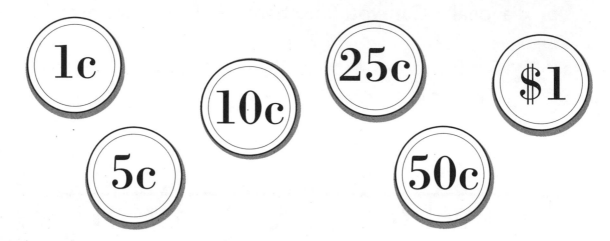

SEE ANSWER 16

PUZZLE 29

Each of the four names below have their vowels missing. Who are they and what is their link?

A) KNNDY

B) SNHWR

C) LNCLN

D) RSVLT

SEE ANSWER 49

PUZZLE 30

Which two digits will replace the question marks?

7	8	5	3
5	0	6	4
2	7	8	9
2	2	7	5
?	?	1	4

SEE ANSWER 8

PUZZLE 31

This grid contains three sports all spelled in the correct order, but mixed with the other two. Which are they?

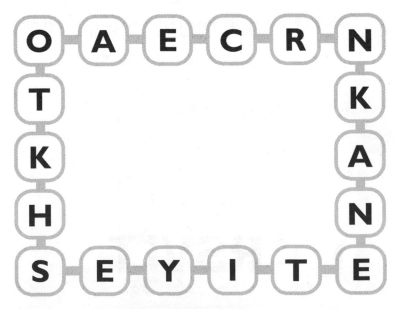

SEE ANSWER 57

55

PUZZLE 32

The codes for these letters are shown below:

A	⊙		G	⊙		O	⊙
B	⊙		H	⊙		P	⊙
C	⊙		I	⊙		R	⊙
D	⊙		L	⊙		S	⊙
E	⊙		M	⊙		T	⊙
F	⊙		N	⊙		U	⊙

Who are these famous historical scientists?

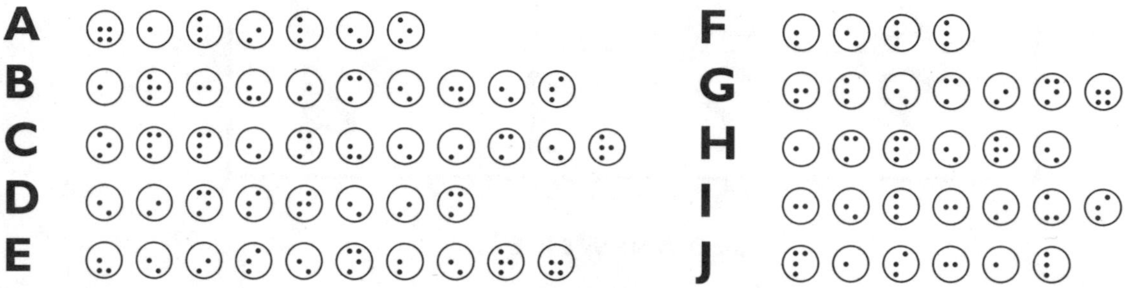

A ⊙⊙⊙⊙⊙⊙ F ⊙⊙⊙⊙

B ⊙⊙⊙⊙⊙⊙⊙⊙⊙ G ⊙⊙⊙⊙⊙⊙⊙

C ⊙⊙⊙⊙⊙⊙⊙⊙⊙⊙⊙ H ⊙⊙⊙⊙⊙⊙

D ⊙⊙⊙⊙⊙⊙⊙ I ⊙⊙⊙⊙⊙⊙

E ⊙⊙⊙⊙⊙⊙⊙⊙⊙ J ⊙⊙⊙⊙⊙⊙

SEE ANSWER 7

PUZZLE 33

Each same letter in this grid has the same value.
Which number should replace the question mark and
what is the value of each letter?

A	B	B	A	**30**
C	C	A	B	**?**
A	A	B	C	
A	C	C	A	

    26   **33**

SEE ANSWER 58

Starting from the top left corner, follow the arrows in a continuous down and up route. Which direction, north, south, east or west, should go in the empty space?

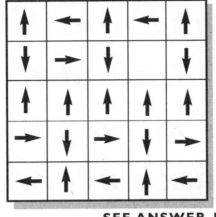

SEE ANSWER 15

PUZZLE 35

5A	4E	2B	1E		1C	4D	5C	1B	4B
□	□	□	□	□	□	□	□	□	□
1D	3D	1E	1C		1B	3A	4C	4E	1E

The wordframe above, when filled with the correct letters, gives the name of a famous boxer. However, to make things interesting you have to decide which letters from the grid below are correct.

	A	B	C	D	E
1	G	R	T	J	E
2	P	K	C	B	W
3	Y	X	F	I	H
4	U	N	Z	A	O
5	M	D	S	V	L

SEE ANSWER 50

LEVEL • MEDIUM

PUZZLE 36

A train travels on an outward journey at 100 miles per hour before returning over the same distance at an average speed of 40 miles per hour. What is the train's average speed over the total journey?

SEE ANSWER 23

PUZZLE 37

Scales 1 and 2 are in perfect balance.
How many diamonds will balance scale 3?

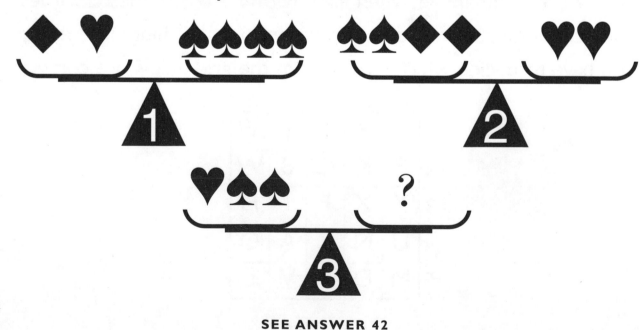

SEE ANSWER 42

Which of these is not a view of the same box?

A
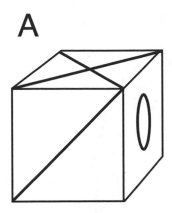

B
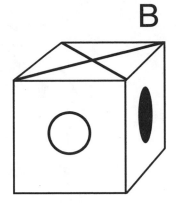

C
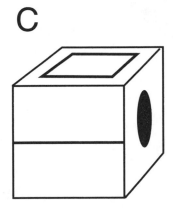

D

E
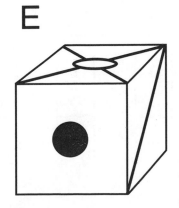

F
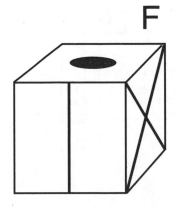

SEE ANSWER 34

LEVEL • MEDIUM

59

PUZZLE 39

Which number should replace the question
mark in the bottom sector?

SEE ANSWER 31

PUZZLE 40

Arrange these pieces to form a square where the
numbers read the same horizontally and vertically.
What will the finished square look like?

| 8 | 6 | 4 |

| 4 | 7 | 6 |

| 3 |
| 8 |

| 0 |
| 8 |
| 5 |

| 3 |
| 5 |

| 3 |
| 3 |

| 1 |
| 5 |
| 4 |

| 7 |
| 6 |

| 2 | 6 |

| 5 |
| 2 |
| 0 |

SEE ANSWER 26

PUZZLE 41

There is a simple logic to the numbers in and around these triangles. Which numbers should replace the question marks?

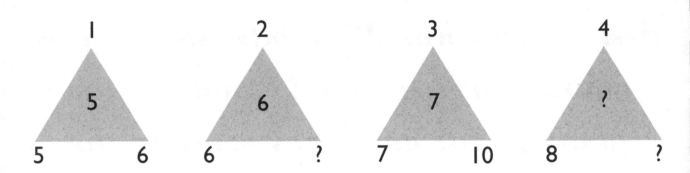

SEE ANSWER 39

PUZZLE 42

This is an unusual safe. Top open it you must press the OPEN button, but you must press all the other buttons in the correct order. This can only be done by following the directions and the number of steps to be taken. Which is the first button you should push?

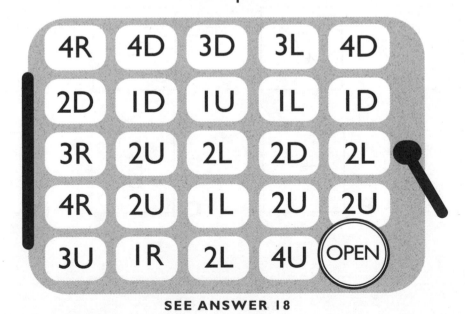

SEE ANSWER 18

PUZZLE 43

In a basketball game, the number of points scored by the home team in the first quarter was 27 points. In the next quarter they scored 21 points. How many points must they score in the second half to average 28 points per quarter over the whole game?

SEE ANSWER 47

PUZZLE 44

Which box follows the shapes in the first three boxes?

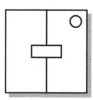 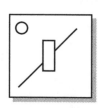 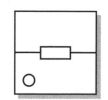

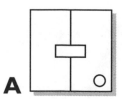
A

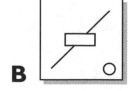
B

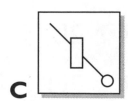
C

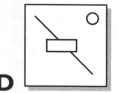
D

SEE ANSWER 10

PUZZLE 45

The hands on these clocks move in a strange but logical way.
What is the time on the fourth clock?

SEE ANSWER 55

PUZZLE 46

A group of five children grabbed a handful of chocolates from a jar. Arnold had seven more chocolates in his hand than Beatrice, and Beatrice had six chocolates less than Claudia. Edgar had three more than David and Claudia had one more than Edgar. Beatrice and Edgar had nine chocolates between them. How many chocolates did the five children have in total?

SEE ANSWER 2

This is an unusual maze. There are a few ways of completing it, but the aim is to collect as few points as possible. What is the lowest possible score?

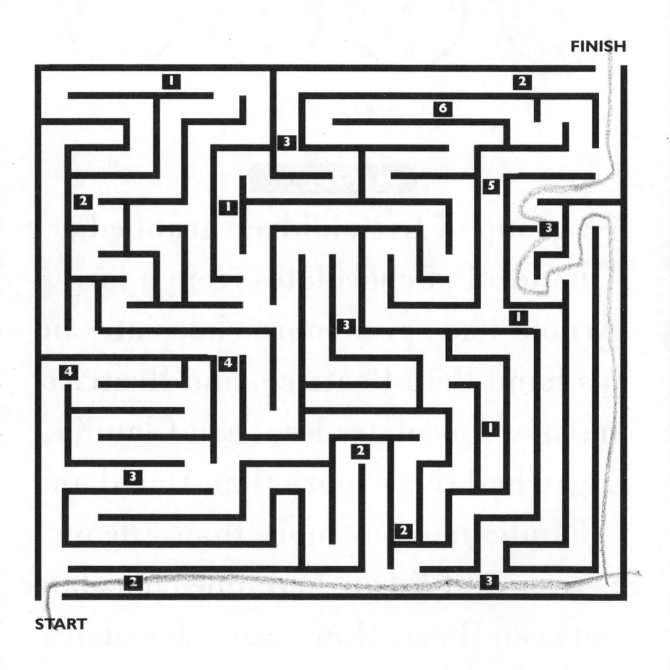

FINISH

START

PUZZLE 48

You have three darts to throw at this dartboard. All must land in a segment to score – even 0 – and none can miss. Although more than one dart can land in the same segment only one order for each set of three can count. How many different ways are there to score 32?

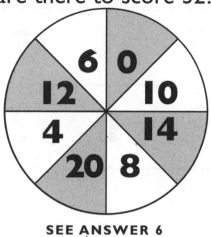

SEE ANSWER 6

PUZZLE 49

Madonna's fan club has 1500 members, Mariah Carey's fan club is 1101 strong and there are 1201 Metallica fans. How many members are there in Michael Jackson's fan club?

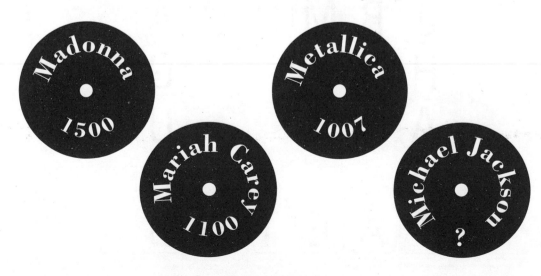

SEE ANSWER 51

PUZZLE 50

Which numbers replace the question marks?

4	7	4	9	5
8	5	1	3	6
3	7	6	?	?

SEE ANSWER 14

PUZZLE 51

The names of one former baseball star and one former football star have been hidden in this frame. Who are they?

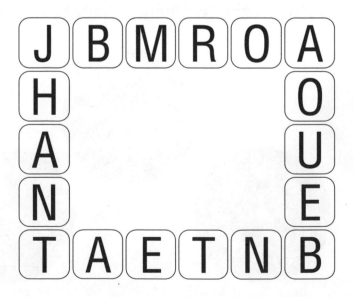

SEE ANSWER 43

PUZZLE 52

Each same symbol has the same value in this grid. Which number replaces the question mark and what are their values?

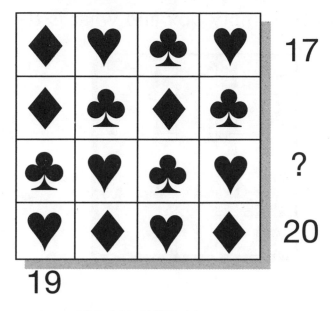

17

?

20

19

SEE ANSWER 22

PUZZLE 53

This clock was correct at midnight (A), but lost one minute per hour from that moment on. It stopped one hour ago (B), having run for less than 24 hours. What is the time now?

A　　　　　**B**

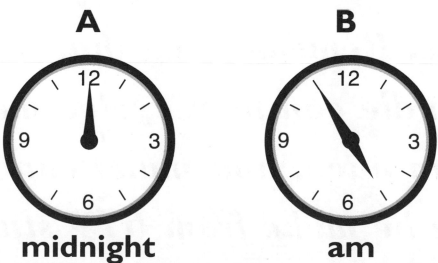

midnight　　　　**am**

SEE ANSWER 35

PUZZLE 54

The arrows from this grid go from the top left corner in a logical sequence. In which direction should the arrow go in the empty box and what is the order?

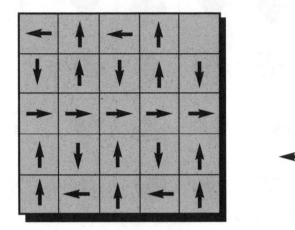

N

SEE ANSWER 30

PUZZLE 55

A man recycles old candles, and can make a new one from 7 stubs. Remembering that a used candle can be recycled more than once, how many candles can he make from 679 stubs?

SEE ANSWER 27

PUZZLE 56

Which numbers replace the question marks?

A	5	3	10	6	15	?	20
B	3	6	?	15	21		
C	2	6	?	54	162	486	

SEE ANSWER 38

PUZZLE 57

Scales 1 and 2 are in perfect balance.
How many stars are required to balance scale 3?

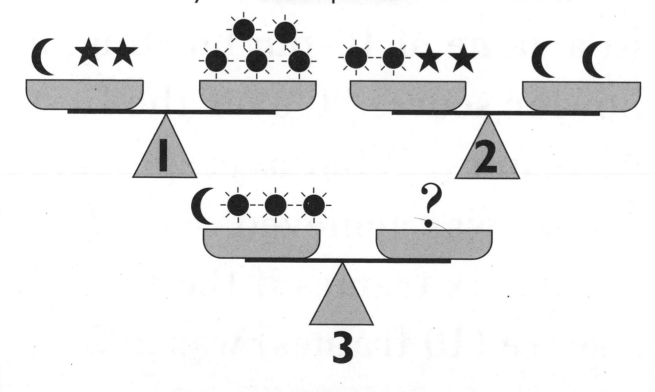

SEE ANSWER 19

PUZZLE 58

Which of these is not a view of the same box?

A

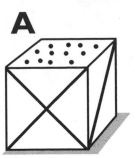

B

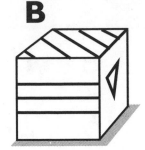

C

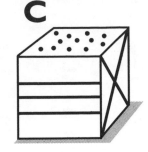

D

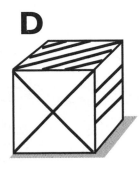

E

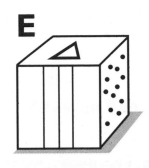

F

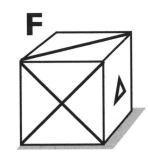

SEE ANSWER 46

PUZZLE 59

In a game of 10-pin bowling, a bowler scores 90 over the first 4 frames. What average pin score was achieved over the next six frames if the final score (10 frames) was 222?

SEE ANSWER 11

PUZZLE 60

Which number should replace the question mark?

SEE ANSWER 54

PUZZLE 61

The hands on these clocks move in a strange but logical way.
What time should replace the question mark?

SEE ANSWER 3

PUZZLE 1

Four of the following numbers have something in common.
What is different about the other one?

6006   5304   2613
5697   8211

SEE ANSWER 57

PUZZLE 2

Look at these parts of the body. They all have something in common except one. Which is it?

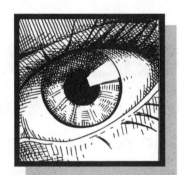
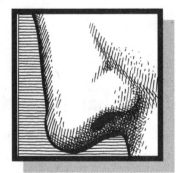

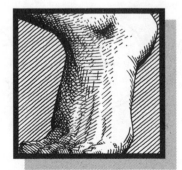

SEE ANSWER 4

In this grid you will find the name of one of the States of the USA jumbled up. Which is it?

SEE ANSWER 49

PUZZLE 4

What has 21 spots but is never ill?

SEE ANSWER 12

PUZZLE 5

Each shape has a value. Scales 1 and 2 are in perfect balance.
How many squares are needed to balance scale 3?

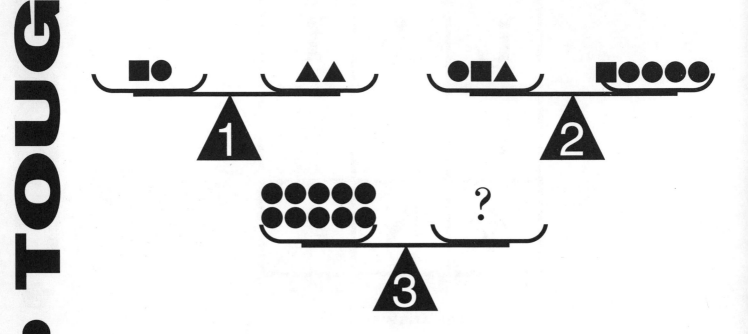

SEE ANSWER 41

PUZZLE 6

What price is the canned fruit in this unusual store in Canada?

Tomato sauce	10c
Orange juice	50c
Iceberg lettuce	30c
Bottled water	$2.10
Canned fruit	?

SEE ANSWER 20

Arrange the pieces to form a square where the numbers read the same vertically and horizontally. What will the finished square look like?

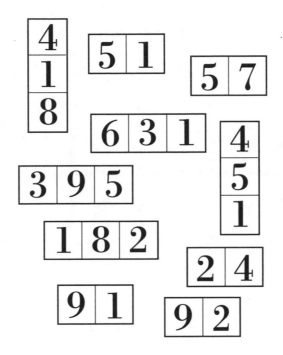

SEE ANSWER 33

PUZZLE 8

What is the price of the dresser in this Welsh furniture store?

Table	£11
Wardrobe	£15
Desk	£1
Sofa	£14
Dresser	£?

SEE ANSWER 28

Each shape in the diagram has a value. Work out the values to discover what number should replace the question mark.

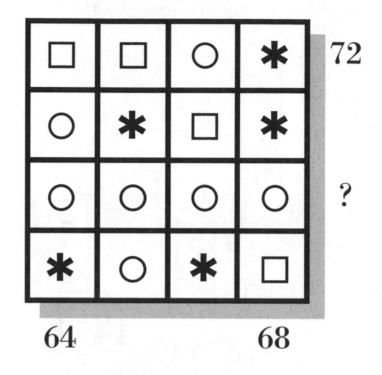

72

?

64   68

SEE ANSWER 25

Each shape has a value. Scales 1 and 2 are in perfect balance.
How many squares are needed to balance scale 3?

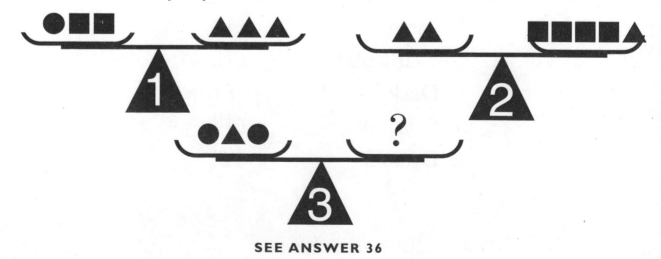

SEE ANSWER 36

PUZZLE 11

The minute and hour hands are moving separately on these weird clocks. What time will the fourth clock show?

SEE ANSWER 17

PUZZLE 12

Start at the far left circle and move, to the rightly only, along the lines to the far right circle, collecting numbers and ovals as you go. Each oval has a value of −10. Each square has a value of −15. What are the minimum and maximum totals possible?

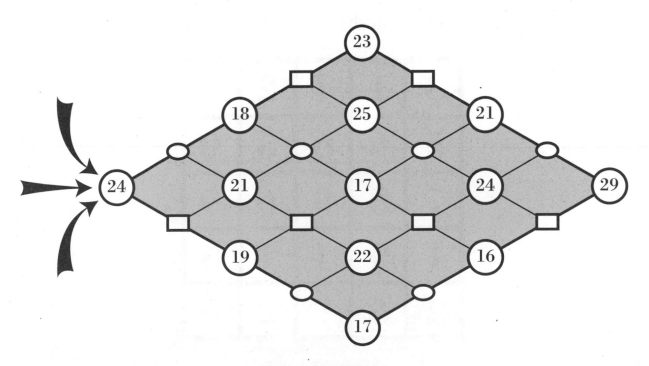

SEE ANSWER 44

PUZZLE 13

Which two boxes in the diagram are alike?

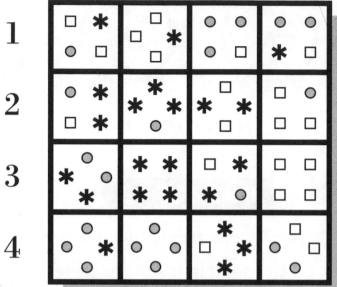

SEE ANSWER 9

PUZZLE 14

What number should replace the question mark?

3	1	4	2	7
5	6	6	5	0
7	8	9	6	9
1	9	4	1	5
2	6	?	2	5

SEE ANSWER 52

78

These sets of numbers all follow logical patterns.
Which numbers replace the question marks?

A) 1, 8, ?, 64, 125

B) 9, 13, 15, ?, 21, 25

C) 00001, 00011, 00101, ?, 01001

D) 17, 23, ?, 18, 20, 25, 21, 9, 15, 16

SEE ANSWER 1

PUZZLE 16

How many triangles are in this shape?

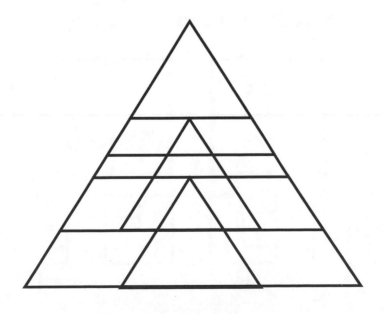

SEE ANSWER 60

PUZZLE 17

Each shape in the diagram has a value. Work out the values to discover what number should replace the question mark.

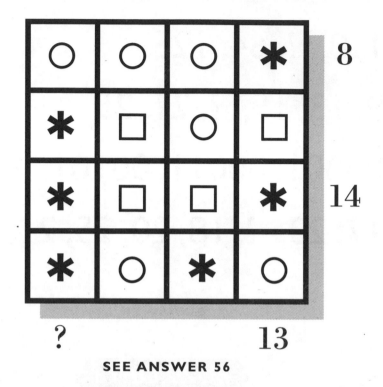

SEE ANSWER 56

PUZZLE 18

Should A, B, C or D come next in this series?

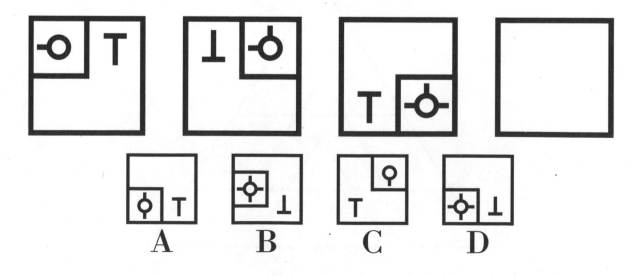

A   B   C   D

SEE ANSWER 3

Here is an unusual safe. Each button must be pressed once only, in the correct order, to reach "Open". The direction to move, i for in, o for out, c for clockwise and a for anti-clockwise (or counterclockwise) is marked on each button. The number of spaces to move is also shown on each button. Which button is the first you must press?

SEE ANSWER 11

81

LEVEL · TOUGH

PUZZLE 20

What number should replace the question mark?

6	7	4	8
2	3	0	0
4	5	2	4
5	6	3	?

SEE ANSWER 48

PUZZLE 21

Which of these is not a view of the same box?

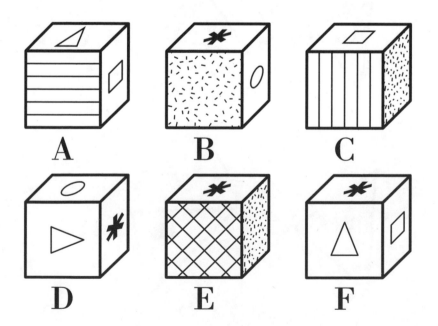

A   B   C

D   E   F

SEE ANSWER 19

Start at the far left circle and move, to the rightly only, along the lines to the far right circle, collecting numbers and ovals as you go. Each oval means divide by 2, each square means multiply by 3, and each triangle means add 13. What are the maximum and minimum totals possible?

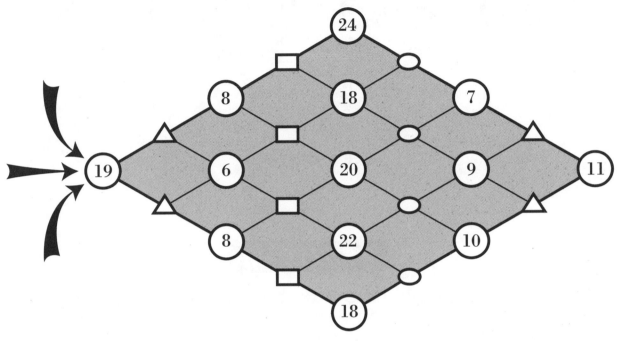

SEE ANSWER 40

The prices in a bakery in England are shown here.
How much should a roll cost?

Bap	35 p
Cake	50 p
Pie	40 p
Roll	?

SEE ANSWER 27

LEVEL · TOUGH

83

PUZZLE 24

Time is moving strangely again on these clocks. What time should the fourth clock show?

1   2   3   4

SEE ANSWER 32

PUZZLE 25

What number should be on the bottom line in this diagram?

8	6	5	3	6
5	1	5	2	4
3	5	0	1	2
1	6	5	1	2
?	?	?	?	?

SEE ANSWER 35

What numbers should surround the fourth triangle?

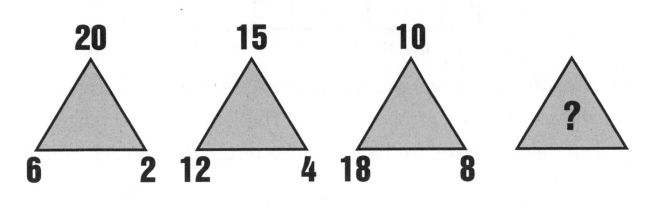

SEE ANSWER 24

PUZZLE 27

Assume you are using a basic calculator and press these numbers in order. Replace each question mark with a mathematical sign. Plus, minus, divide and multiply may be used, but no sign may be used more than once. In which order must they be used?

3?2?1?4?3=1

SEE ANSWER 43

LEVEL • TOUGH

2B	1B	2E	3A	3C	5C	2D	1A
3E	4A	3D	1D	1B	4E	1C	4B

The wordframe above, when filled with the correct letters, will give the name of a Caribbean island. The letters are arranged in the grid below. There are two possible letters to fill each square of the wordframe, one correct, the other incorrect.

What is the island?

	A	B	C	D	E
1	H	A	O	B	F
2	V	B	W	T	R
3	E	U	K	M	J
4	U	S	P	A	I
5	G	Z	D	G	X

SEE ANSWER 16

PUZZLE 29

Which of these is not a view of the same box?

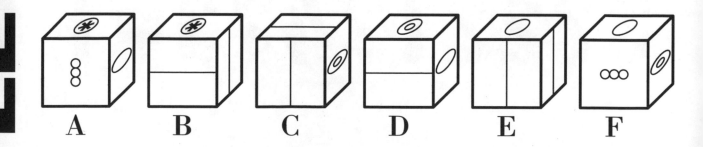

A   B   C   D   E   F

SEE ANSWER 51

LEVEL · TOUGH

PUZZLE 30

How much does a Tequila cost in this strange New York bar?

Vodka	$0.80
Brandy	$1.10
Whiskey	$1.20
Rum	$0.50
Tequila	$?

SEE ANSWER 8

PUZZLE 31

There is only one way to open this safe. You must press each button once only, in the correct order, to reach "Open". Each button is marked with a direction, U for up, L for left, R for right, and D for down. The number of spaces to move is also marked on each button.

Which is the first button you must press?

4D	4D	1L	3L	OPEN
2R	1D	1U	2L	4L
4R	1L	2D	1U	2L
4R	2R	2L	1D	2U
4R	1U	1U	4U	4U

SEE ANSWER 59

LEVEL • TOUGH

PUZZLE 32

On an exercise, a soldier marches for four days. On the first day, he covers 25 per cent of the journey. On the second day, he covers one-third of the remaining distance, on the third, 25 per cent of the remaining journey and, on the final day, he covers half of the remaining distance. He still has 15 miles left to travel. How far has he walked in total?

SEE ANSWER 2

PUZZLE 33

You have three darts to throw at this strange dartboard. Each dart must score and more than one dart can land in the same segment, but separate scoring rounds may not contain the same three values in a different order. How many different ways are there to score 32?

SEE ANSWER 55

Peter has a piggy bank in which there is $40.25, made up of an equal number of each of four coins from 1c, 5c, 10c, 25c, 50c and $1. Which four coins were in the piggy bank and how many of each were there?

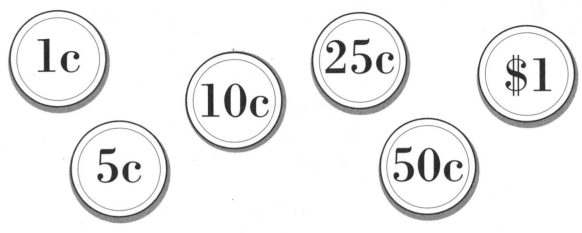

SEE ANSWER 10

PUZZLE 35

The distances on this signpost to the Great Lakes have something to do with their names. What is the distance to Lake Superior?

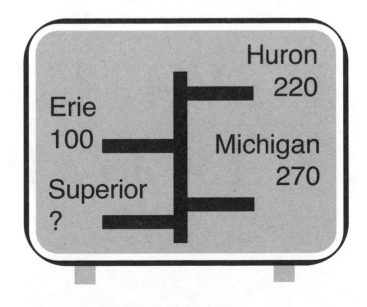

SEE ANSWER 47

LEVEL • TOUGH

89

The clocks move in a special way. What time should be on the blank face?

SEE ANSWER 18

PUZZLE 37

These series of numbers are completely logical. What numbers should replace the question marks in each series?

A) I, IV, VII, ?, XIII
B) 7, ?, 13, 17, 19, 23

SEE ANSWER 39

LEVEL · TOUGH

PUZZLE 38

Which two numbers should replace the question marks?

SEE ANSWER 26

PUZZLE 39

Which numbers should replace the question marks?

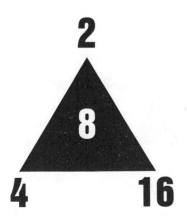

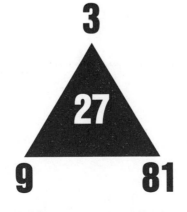

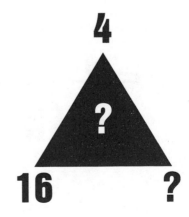

SEE ANSWER 31

A plane covers the first quarter of its journey in 6 hours. In the next 4 hours, it covers one third of the remaining journey and it still has 4,000 miles to go. How far will the total journey be and what has been its average speed so far?

SEE ANSWER 34

PUZZLE 41

Scales 1 and 2 are in perfect balance. How many pairs of cherries will balance scale 3?

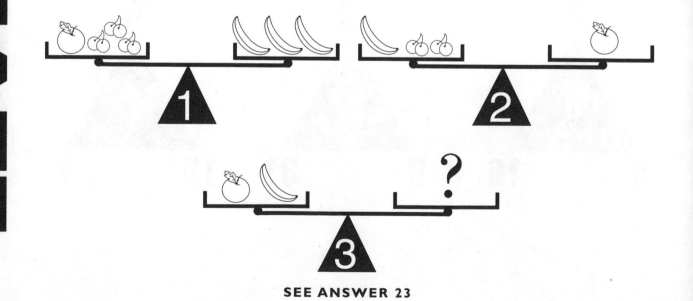

SEE ANSWER 23

LEVEL · TOUGH

PUZZLE 42

Michael Jackson =

Paul McCartney =

If the semaphore codes above are for Michael Jackson and
Paul McCartney, who are the people shown below?

1

2

3

4

5

SEE ANSWER 42

PUZZLE 43

Each like symbol in the diagram has the same value – one of
which is a negative number. Can you work out the logic
and discover which number should replace the question
mark and the values of the symbols?

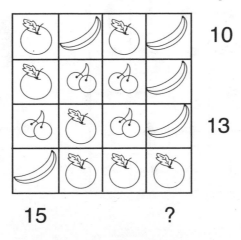

10

13

15   ?

SEE ANSWER 15

PUZZLE 44

This clock was correct at midnight (A), but began to lose one and a half minutes per hour from that moment. It stopped half an hour ago (B), having run for less than 24 hours. What is the correct time now?

A

midnight

B

pm

SEE ANSWER 50

PUZZLE 45

This grid of compass directions follows a set pattern in a continuous horizontal line. What direction is missing and what is the order?

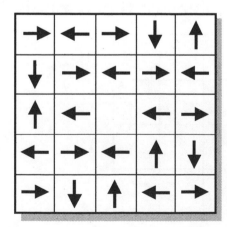

N

SEE ANSWER 7

There is more than one way to complete this maze, so the aim is to complete it by collecting as few points as possible. What is the route and how many points are collected?

LEVEL • TOUGH

SEE ANSWER 58

PUZZLE 47

Here is another unusual safe. To reach the OPEN button, all
the other buttons must be pressed in the correct order.
Each button has a compass direction together with the number
of steps needed. Which is the first button you must press?

4SE	1E	4S	1SE	4SW
2S	1E	1NE	1SE	1SW
1E	1NW	OPEN	2NW	2W
3E	3NE	1SW	3NW	1SW
2N	1N	1N	3N	1N

SEE ANSWER 61

PUZZLE 48

There is a different symbol on each side of the box. Which of
these is not a view of the same box?

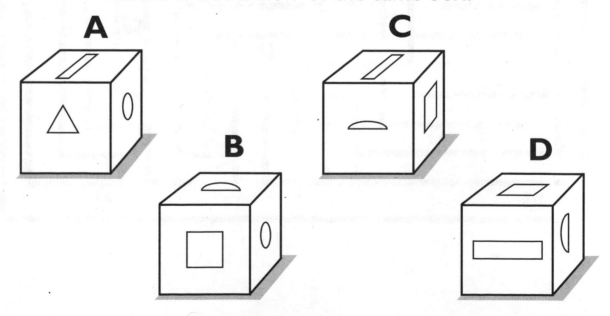

A   **C**   **B**   **D**

SEE ANSWER 6

PUZZLE 49

Over a soccer season, Annie scored 22 more goals than Brenda and Brenda scored 19 less than Carrie. Erica scored 2 more goals than Diana and Carrie scored 15 more than Erica. Brenda and Erica scored 6 goals between them. How many goals did the five players score between them over the season and what is the total?

SEE ANSWER 53

PUZZLE 50

These clocks move in a logical fashion.
What is the time on the blank face?

SEE ANSWER 14

LEVEL • TOUGH

97

PUZZLE 51

Can you use all 9 digits – 1, 2, 3, 4, 5, 6, 7, 8 and 9, in any order – in such a way as to make a fraction equal to one-third?

SEE ANSWER 45

PUZZLE 52

Here is the alphabet with some letters omitted. When you found all the missing ones, they will spell the name of a German city. What is it?

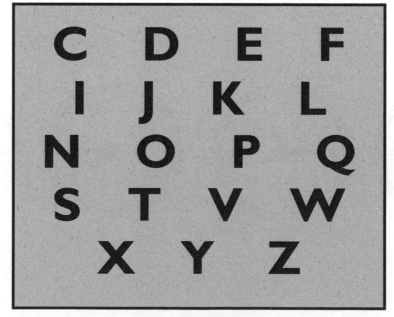

SEE ANSWER 22

At the fair, you have to throw three pebbles to land on these markers. Each pebble must count and more than one can land on the same marker, but the same three markers in a different order does not count. How many ways are there to score 24?

SEE ANSWER 37

There is a logic to the numbers of tourists who visited these cities one day. How many tourists went to Denver that day and how are the numbers worked out?

1	DALLAS	600
2	CHICAGO	201
3	ORLANDO	550
4	DENVER	?

SEE ANSWER 30

LEVEL ○ TOUGH

Which number is the odd one out?

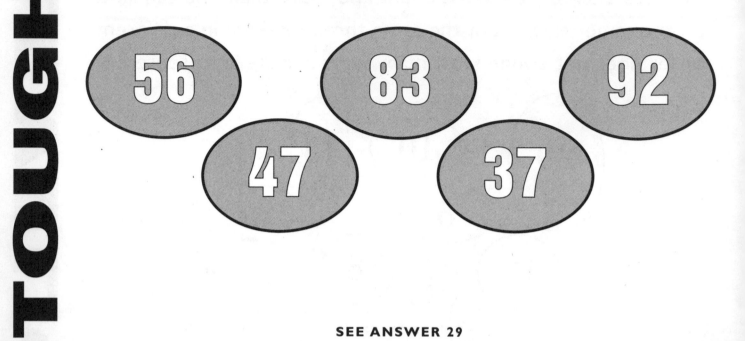

SEE ANSWER 29

PUZZLE 56

Jan has a piggy bank in which there is $12.04, made up of an equal number of each of four coins from 1c, 5c, 10c, 25c, 50c and $1. Which four coins were in the piggy bank and how many of each were there?

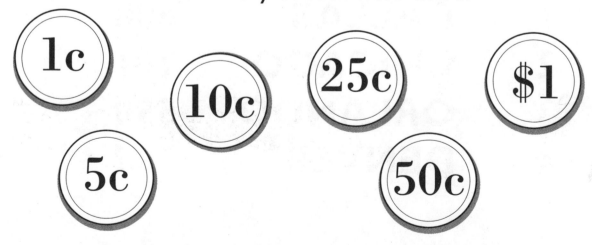

SEE ANSWER 38

LEVEL·TOUGH

100

The ten longest rivers in Europe are hidden in this grid. Each is spelled in a straight line with no letters missed nor any gaps, up, down, across or diagonally, forward or backward.
Can you find them? They are:

Danube   Elbe   Loire   Rhine   Seine
Ebro   Guandiana   Meuse   Rhone   Tagus

G	X	R	V	F	S	H	P	L	A
D	A	N	U	B	E	Q	F	Z	K
R	P	N	E	N	I	H	R	W	Q
C	Y	F	A	J	N	M	F	J	D
Z	K	E	B	I	E	B	I	E	H
E	B	M	B	U	D	G	E	T	H
R	D	U	S	R	Y	N	Q	V	F
I	Z	E	Q	W	O	J	A	P	X
O	N	P	J	H	T	A	G	U	S
L	Y	G	R	X	V	N	N	B	G

SEE ANSWER 21

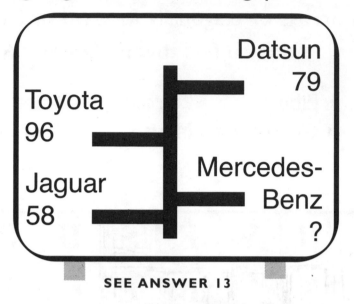 on the left margin, vertically: **LEVEL • TOUGH**

PUZZLE 58

Can you tell how far it is to the Mercedes-Benz garage on this weird signpost?

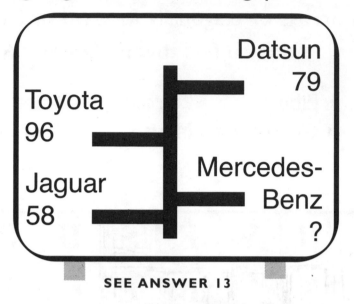

Datsun 79

Toyota 96

Jaguar 58

Mercedes-Benz ?

SEE ANSWER 13

PUZZLE 59

Each same symbol in the diagram has the same value – one of which is a negative number. Can you work out the logic and discover which number should replace the question mark and the values of the symbols?

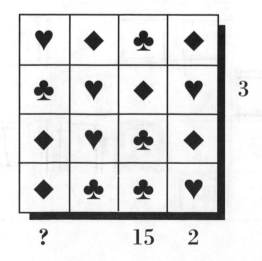

3

?   15   2

SEE ANSWER 46

PUZZLE 60

This clock was correct at midnight (A), but began to lose 4 minutes per hour from that moment. It stopped 2½ hours ago (B), having run for less than 24 hours. What is the correct time now?

A  **B**

midnight   pm

SEE ANSWER 5

10:36

PUZZLE 61

The arrows in this grid go in a clockwise spiral starting from the top left corner. In which direction should the missing arrow point?

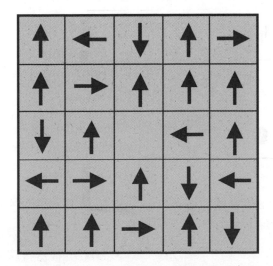

N

SEE ANSWER 54

1. 7.10. The clock moves 15, 20 and 25 minutes forward.

2.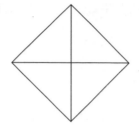

3. 3D in column 1 on row 2.

4. A.

5. 4.

6. A Emerald. This is a stone. The others are metals.
   B Fox. The others are all breeds of pet dogs.

7. A 65. The others are all muliples of 20.
   B 400. The other numbers are multiples of 27.

8. 1 Should I sail
   2 Did Ray smile
   3 Sheila said yes
   4 Museum has old dolls
   5 She sells seashells

9. Andrew is 1 year old.
   The ages relate to the alphabetic position of the first letter of each child's name.

10. C.

11. A DRK. The others are all colours, but DRK is dark.
    B BDMNTN. The others are all sports which use a ball. Badminton uses a shuttlecock.

12. GARDEN. Odd ones out are: Group (others are singles), Almond (others are plants), Rain (others are seasons), Dark (others are light), End (others are start), Nail (others are kitchen implements).

13. C.

14. 44. Add the three outer numbers together, double them and put the answer in the middle.

15.
A	B	K	A	Y	N	E	H
R	E	G	I	T	T	P	A
L	A	K	N	B	O	A	M
I	R	A	T	U	O	M	S
O	H	E	K	I	T	O	T
N	S	N	G	A	G	L	E
P	I	G	O	D	E	E	R
M	F	G	A	M	A	L	L
E	S	O	O	M	V	B	E

16. 8. Add the first row to the second row to give the third row.

17. A Draw Pencil
    B Hot Warm

18. Boiled egg. It is the only one you (probably) wouldn't eat for dinner!

19. Left to right: 24, 24, 25, 23. ★ = 7, ● = 6, ■ = 5.

20. 1. Subtract the top row from the middle row to give the bottom row.

21. Boris Becker and Andre Agassi.

22.

6	8	1	2	4
8	0	9	5	2
1	9	9	6	7
2	5	6	5	1
4	2	7	1	3

23. B.

24. Elephant. All the others are meat-eating animals.

25. 4 ways.

26. 12.30. Each clock moves forward 1 hour and 10 minutes.

27.

28. 21. ★ = 5, ● = 4, ■ = 8.

29. C.

30. A   695. The other numbers have the same first and third digits.

B   10. The numbers double each time and this should be 16.

31. 6. Subtract the two bottom numbers from the top number to give the middle number.

32.

2	4	7	3	1
4	6	0	5	1
7	0	1	2	4
3	5	2	6	8
1	1	4	8	9

33. C.

34. The words contain a fish: CARPet, CODes, sPIKEd, SOLEmn.

35. Birmingham.

36. A   Cuttlee, spelling lettuce. The others are all fruits.

B   Ails, spelling Lisa. The others all spell boys' names.

C   Petal, spelling plate. The others all spell eating implements.

37. £24. Consonants are worth £5, vowels are worth £2.

38. Nein. The others are "yes" in European languages. Nein is "no" in German.

39. A   Happy Birthday to you.

B   There is a drawing pin on the teacher's chair.

40. A 26. Multiples of 6 should make it 24.
B   689. The other numbers' digits increase by two.

41. I am 30.

42. A 33. Each number rises by 9.
B   16. The squares of 1, 2, 3, 4 and 5.

43. x ÷ − +

44. 20. Each vowel is worth 10.

45. A4 and D1.

46. 4. ÷ + x −, or − ÷ + x.

47. A 8 rows of three rabbits
B   28 rows of two rabbits
C   6 rabbits in three rows of three rabbits can be done like these:

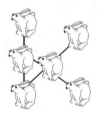 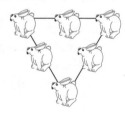

48. A4 and D1.

49.

50. B.

51. 9.

52. Maximum is 59, minimum is 50.

53. Grandmother.

55. 31. It is the only odd number.

54. 2. Subtract the second row from the top row to give the bottom row.

56. A 11. The numbers reduce by 1, 2, 3, 4, 5 and 6.
B   9. The number increases by 3 each time.

57. 13. ★ = 3, ● = 2, ■ = 5.

58. B1 and A3.

59. 1i in the outer circle, between 1i and 1c.

60. Venezuela.

61. 5.05. The clock moves forward 1 hour and 25 minutes each time.

62. 10. The alphbetic position of the first letter multiplied by 10.

63. Move the top star to below the bottom row. Move the two outside stars on the bottom row to become the outside two on the new top row.

64. Switzerland

SOLUTIONS TO MEDIUM PUZZLES

3. Rembrandt
4. Donatello
5. Ernst
6. van Gogh

1. 15. Double the number, then add 1.

2. 30. Arnold had 9 chocolates, Beatrice 2, Claudia, 8, David 4 and Edgar 7.

3. 2.45. The hour hand moves forward 2 hours each time, the minute hand moves alternately forward 5 minutes and back 10.

4. $7. The difference between the alphebetic positions of the first and second letters of each animal gives the cost.

5. 5.25. In each case, the hour hand moves forward by 5 hours and the minute hand forward by 20 minutes.

6. 8 ways.

7.
A   Galileo
B   Archimedes
C   Oppenheimer
D   Einstein
E   Heisenberg
F   Bell
G   Fleming
H   Ampere
I   Celsius
J   Pascal

8. 0 and 5. Subtract the lower line from the one immediately above it and put the answer directly below.

9.
1. Monet
2. Dali

10. C. The circle moves 90° anti(counter) clockwise, the straight line moves 45° clockwise and the rectangle moves 90° clockwise.

11. 22.

12. 3. In each row, subtract the middle number from the left to give the right.

13. 20. ★ = 2, ● = 4, ■ = 7

14. 4 and 1. Add the top line to the bottom line to give the middle line.

15. East.

16. 4 each of $1, 25c, 5c and 1c.

17. Glockenspiel.

18. 2U on row 4 in column 4.

19. 4 stars.

20. Beethoven.

21. 7. It is run of consecutive prime numbers.

22. 14. Diamond = 6, Heart = 4, Club = 3.

23. 57.14 miles per hour.

24. 4A and 4D.

25. 4 ways.

26.

1	5	4	7	6
5	2	0	3	3
4	0	8	5	8
7	3	5	2	6
6	3	8	6	4

27. 113 candles.

28. 10.50. The time moves backwards 1 hour, 5 minutes on each clock.

29. 1 and 6. On each row, add the two outer numbers to give the middle one.

30. West. The order is West, South, East, North, North, and it runs continuously down column 1, up column 2, down column 3, etc.

31. 10. The numbers in each sector are added together and the diagonally opposite sectors have the same total.

32. Hour hand on 6, minute hand on 5 to the hour. In each case the minute hand goes back 20 minutes and the hour hand 1 hour forward.

33. 104. Multiply the alphabetic position of the first and last letters of each place.

34. E.

35. 6.00 am.

36. $49.00. Each consonant has a value of $5 and a vowel $8, and they are added together.

37. 18. ★ = 6, ● = 5, ■ = 4.

38. A   9. Subtract 2, add 7, subtract 4, add 9, subtract 6 and add 11.
     B   10. Add 3, 4, 5 and 6.
     C.   18. Multiply each number by 3.

39. The numbers at the top, middle and left are consecutive. The top and left numbers are then added together to give the right number.

8   12

40. 12.31 miles per hour.

41.

N	B	W	R	Y	A	V	M	D	A
X	E	J	V	D	H	A	O	I	C
H	B	W	A	C	R	K	N	A	F
Y	D	V	M	I	T	R	T	K	G
K	E	F	Z	E	O	W	A	S	N
N	Q	O	X	F	X	Q	N	A	I
B	N	A	I	G	P	I	A	L	M
A	S	L	H	C	B	F	C	A	O
P	A	J	N	O	G	E	R	O	Y
C	O	L	O	R	A	D	O	G	W

42. 3 diamonds.

43. Babe Ruth and Joe Montana.

44. 48. Add together the bottom two numbers, multiply the total by the top and place the answer in the middle.

45. 15. Add 2, 3, 4, 5 and 6.

46. F.

47. 64.

48. $3.15. Each vowel is worth 60c and each consonant is worth 15c. The values are then all added together.

49. They are all former Presidents of the United States of America. They are:
A   Kennedy
B   Eisenhower
C   Lincoln
D   Roosevelt

50. Mike Tyson.

51. 1,251. The values of the roman numerals in each star's name are added together.

52. D.

53. 2 squares.

54. 10. The three numbers in each sector are added together and the totals in the bottom four segments are double those of their diagonally opposite ones.

55. 8.05. The clocks move 4 hours and 50 minutes forward each time.

56.

9	1	4	6	3
1	2	5	3	1
4	5	8	0	2
6	3	0	9	6
3	1	2	6	7

57. Hockey, Karate and Tennis.

58. 29. A = 11, B = 4, C = 7.

59. 8.

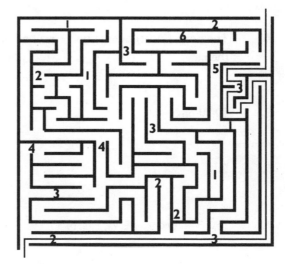

60. 2. In each row, multiply the two out numbers to give the middle one.

61. 4 (26 ways).

1. A) 27. The cubes of 1, 2, 3, 4 and 5.
    B) 19. Consecutive prime numbers from 7 with 2 added each time.
    C) 00111. Alternate numbers on the binary scale.
    D) 5. The alphabetic position of the letters on the top line of a typewriter, Q, W, E, R, T, Y, U, I, O, P.

2. 65 miles.

3. D. The small square moves clockwise with the circle gaining an extra line each time. The T moves anti(counter)-clockwise and rotates through 180°.

4. The nose. (Most) people only have one of them!

5. 10.30 pm.

6. B.

7. East. The order is E, W, E, S, N, W.

8. $1.00. Each consonant is worth 20c and each vowel 10c. The letters are added together.

9. 2A and 3C.

10. 25 each of 1c, 10c, 50c, and $1.

11. 5a in the inner circle.

12. A die (dice).

13. 119. The alphabetic positions of all the letters of the names are added together.

14. 7.45. In each case the clocks move forward 3 hours and 30 minutes.

15. 3. Apples = 6,
        Bananas = −1,
        Cherries = 4.

16. Barbados.

17. 9.15. In each case the hour hand moves forward 1 hour and the minute hand 15 minutes forward.

18. 4.20. The times move forward by 1 hour and 5 minutes, 2 hours and 10 minutes, 4 hours and 20 minutes and 8 hours and 40 minutes.

19. E.

20. 30c. The alphabetic position of the first letters of the two words are subtracted and the value is multiplied by 10 cents.

21.

G	X	R	V	F	$	H	P	L	A
D	A	N	U	B	E	Q	F	Z	K
R	P	N	E	N	I	H	R	W	Q
C	Y	F	A	J	N	M	F	J	D
Z	K	E	B	I	E	B	L	E	H
E	B	M	R	U	D	G	E	T	H
R	D	U	S	R	Y	N	Q	V	F
I	Z	E	Q	W	Q	J	A	P	X
O	N	P	J	H	T	A	G	U	S
L	Y	G	R	X	V	N	N	B	G

22. Hamburg.

23. 7 pairs of cherries.

24.

5

24   16

The right number doubles; the left number goes up by 6 and the top number goes down by 5.

25.   52. ★ = 17, ● = 13, ■ = 21.

26.   Outer 3, inner 9. The numbers in the outer sectors are added together and the sums of the top half are double those of the diagonally opposite bottom halves. The top half numbers in the inner part of the sectors are three times those of the diagonally opposite bottom half ones.

27.   45p. Each vowel is worth 15p, each consonant is worth 10p. They are added together to give the final value.

28.   £5. Each vowel is worth 10 and each consonant is worth −3. These are added together to give the price.

29.   37. The other numbers' digits all add to 11.

30.   505. The roman numerals in each name are added together.

31.   Bottom right = 64, middle = 256.
The left and top numbers are multiplied and the answer is put in the middle. The top and middle numbers are then multiplied and this answer goes to the right.

32.   1.00. In each case, the time is moving back 2 hours 10 minutes.

33.

4	5	1	9	2
5	6	3	1	4
1	3	9	5	1
9	1	5	7	8
2	4	1	8	2

34.   The distance is 8,000 miles and the average speed so far is 400 miles per hour.

35.   18500. Each line is deducted from the the line above to give the line below.

36.   24 squares.

37.   9 ways.

38.   14 each of 1c, 10c, 25c and 50c.

39.   A   X. The values increase by 3 in roman numerals.
            B   11. It is a series of prime numbers.

40.   Minimum is 97, maximum is 105.

41.   2 squares.

42.   1   Phil Collins.
            2   Michael Schumacher.
            3   Sean Connery.
            4   Mike Tyson.
            5   John Lennon.

43. x + − ÷. (3 x 2 [6] + I [7] − 4 [3] ÷ 3 = I).

44. Lowest is 45, highest is 83.

45. $\dfrac{5832}{17496} = \dfrac{1}{3}$

46. 8. Heart = −2, Diamond = 3, Club = 4.

47. 370. Add the alphabetic position of the first and last letters, then multiply by 10.

48. 6. On each row, I is added to the first number to give the second number. Column three has 3 subtracted from column two and column four is double the value of column three.

49. Louisiana.

50. 8.30 pm.

51. E.

52. I. On each row, subtract the two right numbers from the two left ones. The answer is put in the middle.

53. 52 goals. Annie scored 23 goals, Brenda I, Carrie 20, Diana 3, Erica 5.

54. North. The order is N, W, S, N, E, N.

55. 8 ways.

56. 16. ★ = 5, ● = I, ■ = 2.

57. 5697. The units in each of the other numbers, when added together, total 12.

58. The lowest possible scoring route is 9.

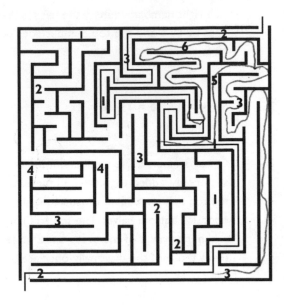

59. IU in row 3 on column 4.

60. 10.

61. IE on row 2, column 2.